Beachbum Berry's

Taboo Table

Tiki Cuisine from Polynesian Restaurants of Yore

By Jeff Berry

Illustration by Kevin Kidney

Published by Club Tiki Press/SLG Publishing
44 Race Street San Jose, CA 95126
All contents tm & © 2013 All rights reserved
www.clubtiki.com   •   www.slgcomic.com

Acknowledgements

Dedicated to Annene Kaye: She had her pick, but she chose a bum.

For building the boat, thanks to Dan Vado, Craig Pape, and Otto Von Stroheim; for charting the course, to Annene, Sven Kirsten, and Bob Van Oosting and Leroy Schmaltz of Oceanic Arts; for such smooth sailing, to Bosko Hrnjak, Kevin Kidney, Scott Saavedra, Truus De Groot, and Martha Kaye; and for safe harbor, to the Tiki-Ti and all who drop anchor there.

Written by Jeff Berry
Art Direction & Layout by Scott Saavedra
Original Illustrations by Kevin Kidney
Published by Dan Vado

Front Cover Diorama by Bosko Hrnjak;
Photographed by Sven Kirsten.

isbn 978-1-59362-247-3

Illustration by Kevin Kidney

Table of Contents

Illustration by Kevin Kidney

Introduction

Polynesian restaurants were phenomenally popular for a large part of the 20th century, even though the conventional wisdom regarding them (wisdom we ourselves have oft repeated) was go for the drinks, go without dinner. In a 1993 review of Ohio's Kahiki restaurant, a *Columbus Monthly* critic raved about the decor, but couldn't find one item on the entire menu that he could recommend; he was particularly affronted by a dish allegedly from the Coral Islands: "The combination of crab meat, cream cheese and beef is just as bad as it sounds ... Apparently in the Coral Islands, food is used as a form of punishment."

So why bother to compile a book of food recipes from the heyday of Polynesian restaurants? Perhaps the answer lies in a sweltering summer night in Hollywood, 1947, when Orson Welles dared remove his dinner jacket inside Don The Beachcomber's dining room. Beachcomber manager Bud Bachtold insisted that Welles put his coat back on again. Welles announced that it was the last time he would ever visit such a stuffy place. "It was the last time," remembered Bachtold, "for a whole week." You see where we're going with this? Welles, as infamous a *gourmand* as an *enfant terrible*, wasn't drinking in the bar, he was eating in the dining room. The question now becomes not how bad Polynesian food could be, but how good.

Don the Beachcomber's restaurant chain survived for half a century, and Trader Vic's empire is still healthy at the age of 66. In the trend-happy, high-turnover American restaurant business, these lifespans are eternities; neither concern could have thrived as long as it did by serving inferior cuisine.

Other mid-century Polynesian restaurants apparently held their own in the food department too, even earning a begrudging endorsement from *Gourmet* magazine in 1958: "If you must eat in the dark amidst papier-mâché waterfalls while Polynesian natives from the University of California graduate schools at Berkeley perform tribal rites with drinks in coconut shells, the fact stands that hidden in the tidewater trash on the menu in many a South Seas deadfall there lurk other dishes of surprising elegance."

Taboo Table aims to do for these dishes what our previous volumes, *Grog Log* and *Intoxical*, did for "drinks in coconut shells." Herein we'll rediscover vintage food recipes from restaurants both famous and forgotten, along with some non-restaurant recipes influenced by the era's obsession with Polynesian food. But before we put on our chef's aprons, we must ask another question: Just what the hell *was* Polynesian food, anyway? Considering that Polynesian restaurants served almost everything under the sun, an easier question might be: What wasn't it?

From Long Pig to Pig Ignorant

Restaurant Polynesia was, with apologies to Lawrence Ferlinghetti, "A Phony Island Of The Mind." A trip to one of these places would have given an anthropologist acute indigestion before eating a bite. But for the average unlettered suburbanite, they were a triumphant fiction. It's no coincidence that Hollywood art directors were often hired to create Polynesian restaurant interiors, the best of which had the same effect on patrons as a good movie -- enveloping them so completely in a fantasy world that, for an evening at least, they escaped their own. Who cared that the dreamlike aura of primitive paradise came courtesy of modern industry, particularly when you were dining in a hidden nook beside the waterfall of a romantic lagoon (molded with Monsanto polysulfide polymer), cooled by soft tropical breezes (circulated by Westinghouse's Radiant Comfort System), guarded by mysterious pagan idols (varnished with Flintkote fire-retardant), to the sound of jungle bird calls (recorded on Ampex Precision Magnetic tape)? So what if the Ceylonese tablecloth was really Celanese-Fortrel? So seductive, so total was the atmosphere, especially to children who were as naive as the decor's cultural perspective, that on his first voyage to the South Seas, the Beachbum actually found himself unfavoringly comparing Polynesia to Polynesian restaurants.

Little did the young Bum know or care that the "Polynesian" cuisine of these restaurants was not South Pacific-specific, but mostly Cantonese fare re-christened with exotic new names. Fried wontons became "Tiki's Nest," Peking duck "Pago Pago Duck," and steamed dumplings "Puka Puka Dim Sims."

This was no mere caprice, but a gastronomic necessity: The food actually consumed in the island paradises of primitive Polynesia wouldn't have rated many stars in the Micheline guide. Breadfruit and taro root were the daily staples, supplemented on special occasions by kelp. "One mouthful was a complete dose," Herman Melville wrote of the "saline salad" offered to him by a Marquesan chief in 1842, "and great was the consternation of the old warrior at the rapidity with which I rejected his Epicurean treat."

True, the Polynesians never lacked for fresh fish. But meat was scarce and, on an island, all-too-easily hunted to extinction. Such was the fate of the Moa, an eleven-foot-tall, wingless bird that pretty much had New Zealand to itself until the Maoris arrived. The first seafarers who migrated into the Polynesian Triangle from southern Asia, populating the islands between 1700 BC and 1000 AD, did bring chickens and pigs with them; but the most interesting meat dish they imported ... was themselves.

While the Hawaiians and Tahitians both practiced human sacrifice, the jury's still out on whether or not they actually ate their victims. No such confusion exists over the Samoans and Marquesans, who, according to Mick Anglo in his book *Man Eats Man*, "ate human flesh because they relished it." The Maoris consumed the eyes of their enemies as an hors d'oeuvre, and the rump fat as a sweet-potato dressing. Touai, a Maori chief who visited London in 1818, bemoaned the lack of Long Pig on British menus; he said he preferred the taste of women and children to adult males, and dark meat to white. The Papuans enjoyed their missionaries roasted, but the Maoris served man *au jus*: stewed in his own juices, with salt to taste.

The missionary pot gave way to the melting pot as 19th-century Hawaii was hit by waves of Chinese, Japanese, Portuguese and Filipino immigration. They all added their native dishes to the mix, creating the original Pacific Rim fusion cuisine. What we have come to regard as the most Hawaiian of foods, the pineapple, was not native to Polynesia; Yankee planters introduced it from Central America in the early 1800s.

Ironically, by the 20th century Hawaiian cuisine was considerably more cosmopolitan than that of the mainland. Aside from the very rich, most Americans didn't see much of the world before jet airliners democratized travel. This cultural isolation brewed culinary mistrust: Before the 1930s, the average citizen rarely ventured into a Chinese restaurant, and only then as a kind of daring lark. Chinese kitchens were widely thought unclean; soy sauce was known as "bug juice." The xenophobia was mutual: Chinese chefs held their ignorant white patrons in contempt, serving them dishes no one in China would touch with a bamboo pole. The most popular entree with Americans, chop suey, was basically stir-fried leftovers. (Invented in New York in 1894, chop suey is a corruption of the Cantonese "shop sui," or "odds and ends.")

Nevertheless, Don The Beachcomber opted for a Cantonese menu when he expanded his bar into a restaurant in 1937. Why? He needed exotic food to accompany his exotic drinks, and back then Cantonese was about as exotic as food got. "Don hired a Chinese cook," recalled Ray Buhen, one of the Beachcomber's original bartenders; "the cook just cooked what he always cooked and we called it something Polynesian. No one knew. It was crazy." The gambit worked, with Don's wife Sunny personally taking customers on guided tours of the spotlessly clean Chinese kitchen.

Chinese restaurant owners, noting Don's success, were not to be outdone: Since they were *already* serving "exotic" Cantonese food, all they had to do was slap some tapa cloth on the walls, dangle some puffer fish from the ceiling, add a tropical drink page to the menu, and presto -- instant Polynesian restaurant! A shining example of this is Yue's, late of Gardena, California, which lined its Ming Dynasty-style exterior with tiki torches to cash in on the craze. Other Chinese restaurateurs, such as Benson Fong of Ah Fong's, were more like hermit crabs: When the Bora Bora room of Encino, California, went bankrupt because it couldn't recoup the costs of its

AH FONG'S

**Family Style
CANTONESE DINNERS**

spectacular Polynesian decor, Fong simply moved in a Cantonese kitchen staff and started raking in the exoticash. (Fong, Charlie Chan's "number one son" in the 1940s movie series, became the number one 1960s Cantonese king with five Ah Fong's restaurants located throughout L.A. County.)

Bora Bora
POLYNESIAN CUISINE

**16240 VENTURA BLVD.
ENCINO, CALIF.**

Trader Vic took the "exotic restaurant" concept a little more seriously. American cities are now bursting at the seams with Japanese, Thai, Indian, Mediterranean, Caribbean, Korean and Indonesian restaurants. But in the 1950s, the first place diners may have encountered dishes from these lands was at Trader Vic's. In addition to the usual Chinese and Continental dishes, Vic introduced sashimi, satays, curries, lavoshes, and spices from Martinique to Malaysia. Vic's son Lynn Bergeron labeled this synthesis of Eastern and Western culture "International Food." Adds restaurant critic Ruth Reichl: "They had a grazing menu before grazing was a concept." It wasn't until the late 1970s -- when the ethnic groups Vic had borrowed from started opening their own restaurants -- that critics turned on the Trader, dismissing as commonplace the same dishes that had surprised them a few years earlier. But, like its hardier competition in the *faux*-Polynesian racket, Trader Vic's survived on the novelty of its rum drinks and the appetizers that soaked them up. Which brings us to the recipes we have resurrected for this book.

TRADER VIC'S

HONOLULU'S ORIGINAL
POLYNESIAN RESTAURANT
• Rum Originals
• Cantonese Food
PH. 57428 • 926 WARD

Pupu Chatter

The appetizer assortment, or pupu platter, was the mainstay of Polynesian restaurant menus. It's not hard to figure out why: Patrons largely came for the liquid refreshment, and if you had a little something to eat, you could have a lot more to drink. To increase capacity, one mid-century bar guide offered these tips for tipplers: "Drink a glass of cream, or eat a thickly buttered piece of bread. Drink a jigger of olive oil, or chew on some not-too-crisp fried bacon. Have a bowl of hot meat soup, heavily buttered." Compared to that, ordering a tray of deep-fried, sugar-glazed, cheese-stuffed tidbits was not only more palatable, but on balance probably less likely to give you arteriosclerosis.

Most pupus were Chinese restaurant standards: egg rolls, spare-ribs, fried shrimp and paper-wrapped chicken. However, Don the Beachcomber did come up with one genuine innovation, Rumaki (recipe on page 34), which enjoyed a 25-year vogue as the most popular Polynesian restaurant appetizer. Don's motive was less culinary than monetary. According to his friend Herb Kane, Don's poultry supplier forced him to buy whole chickens "and Don couldn't stand all of the chicken livers going to waste." Finally he hit on the notion of combining them with water chestnuts and wrapping them in bacon. "He had a Cook Islands dictionary," remembered Kane. "He opened it, his finger came down on the word rumaki, and that's what he called it." Rumaki is actually the name of a Cook Islands bird.

Don the Beachcomber

SAN DIEGO, CALIF.

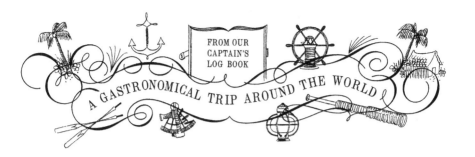
Other Polynesian restaurant chefs eventually created some
equally inventive appetizers of their own -- inventions which
form the bulk of our Appetizer recipe section.

Specialties of the Hut

Polynesian places generally offered a potpourri of entrées:
Chinese food, American standards, and a smattering of *faux-*
Polynesian "signature dishes" -- which mostly involved adding pineapple or coconut to Chinese food and American standards. While the Bum has a greater tolerance for tropical
fruit in his drinks than in his dinner, some of these signature dishes actually work. We put the best of
what we found in the Entrée
recipe section,
along with
a sampler of
Cantonese-
style dishes,
rounded
out by
some of the
"International
Food" first
popularized by
Trader Vic.

Bali Ha'i

CANTONESE / AMERICAN
WORLDWIDE CUISINE
CONTINENTAL / POLYNESIAN

A few of these "International" recipes may have a familiar ring to you. That's because, *a la* the re-named Cantonese dishes, Polynesian restauranteurs were fond of giving Continental menu items exotic new monikers -- but not so exotic that diners couldn't recognize their favorite dishes. This strategy catered to customers who, in the words of mid-century *bon vivant* Lucius Beebe, "admire the Mai Tais at the bar but want Christian food when they sit down at table." Christian food such as "Rapa Nui Lobster Tail," "Steak Genghis Kahn" and, our favorite, "Montea Kristo Ai" (that's Monte Cristo Sandwich to you -- see page 53).

Startling Starts and Flaming Finishes

This practice extended to first and last courses as well: Take a popular "Christian" dish, tweak it, re-name it, and serve it with a side of South Seas showmanship. Forgive us if we sound cynical, because we are most assuredly not: The recipe-tweaking was often as imaginative as the re-naming. Not only that, we happen to like our salads tossed with long tiki-shaped forks and our desserts topped with flaming sauces; Polynesian-style presentation gives an entirely new meaning to "playing with your food." *Do* try this at home after consulting our remaining food-recipe sections: Soups, Salads & Sides, and Desserts.

Luaus and Libations

In the words of Hawaii's ancient chiefs: "Look not with ungracious eyes upon the traveler who passes your door. You must bid him enter. Your pig must be killed. Whoever does not respect this order is to be taken to the public place and shamed." But killing your pig is one thing, and killing yourself is another. That's why the Beachbum has never thrown a luau: Feeding, entertaining, and inebriating a large group of people inevitably leaves you too frazzled to play the proper host. Trader Vic preferred giving dinner parties with up to eight guests, so he could give each one his full attention. The Bum hastens to agree (and, being a bum, he rarely hastens to do anything).

With this in mind, we've freighted our Drinks
section with blender recipes that can serve six
to eight people in one go -- ideal for intimate
cocktail parties, patio barbecues, and other small
gatherings. For larger affairs, we've thrown in some punch-
bowl recipes as well.

A Word About Health

If you value yours, please remember that most of these recipes were in vogue when butter and red meat were at the top
of the food pyramid. Like the Polynesian restaurant ethos
itself, they are all about indulgence, abandon, and casting
your fate to the wind. Rather than sacrifice the richness
that mid-century diners expected when they ate out, we've
chosen to present the recipes pretty much as they were

originally pre-
pared. Where we
have substituted
ingredients, it
wasn't to make
them healthier -
- just tastier. (All
altered recipes
are so indicated
at the bottom of
the page on which
they appear.)

dine in our tropical garden restaurant....celestial chicken — lobster
flamedor — exotic cantonese food
— east indian curries — charcoal
broiled steaks — unusual rum drinks
— "witches brew" — "head hunter"
— "pagan love" — visit our 'round
the world gift shop.

One last caveat: MSG, also known as Ajimoto or Ac'cent, was used liberally by mid-century chefs. It's now known to cause an allergic reaction called "Chinese Restaurant Syndrome" in some people. If you may be one of them, kindly omit the MSG from our recipes that call for it -- it won't kill the flavor, and it just might save you!

Hard-to-find Ingredients

Whenever you come across one in the recipes, turn to our Resource Guide. You'll find ordering information there.

Tricks of the Trade

Here's a run-down of prep and presentation procedures common to many of the *faux*-Polynesian recipes in this book:

COCONUT MILK, COCONUT CREAM, & SHREDDED COCONUT:

Given his aversion to labor, especially of the manual kind, the Bum is pleased to be living in an age when he can obtain all things coconut without actually having to open a coconut. Go for the Thai Kitchen Organic brand of COCONUT MILK, because there's nothing in the can but coconut. However, canned coconut cream (such as Lopez) is meant for drinks only and will *not* work in food recipes. To render coconut cream suitable for cooking, chill an unopened can of coconut milk in the fridge overnight; the milk should congeal, giving you COCONUT CREAM. (We say "should" because organic coconut milk, lacking emulsifiers, may not harden; you might want to skip the suspense and opt for a can containing the guar gum that abets congealing. Or just freeze the can and semi-defrost before use.) As for SHREDDED COCONUT, stow your hammer, your grater, and your temper and just pick up a package of Bob's Red Mill brand (any other brand you buy should be all-natural and, most important, *unsweetened*).

FLAMBÉEING: The trick to successful alcohol ignition is to pre-warm the liquor slowly in a long-handled ladle or, safer still, in a double-boiler (poured into the ladle after warming). Then ignite the liquor in the ladle from a safe distance, using a long-stemmed match. While the flame is burning brightly, carefully pour it over the food -- which should be contained in a chafing dish or heat-resistant platter, on a level surface (*sans* flammable tablecloth, of course).

WHIPPED CREAM: Chill whipping cream first, as warm cream won't always whip. Use an electric mixer, gradually increasing speed as you move the beater across the bottom of the bowl. Serve soon after whipping, before stiffened cream loses its shape again. To make the Beachbum's own RUM WHIPPED CREAM, beat 1/2 cup cream till it peaks, then whisk in 2 teaspoons sugar and 3 teaspoons dark Jamaican rum.

WOODEN SKEWERS: To make sure the wood doesn't burn in the broiler, pre-soak bamboo skewers or toothpicks in cold water for at least 30 minutes. Or, if you're pressed for time, just cover the exposed ends in aluminum foil and remove after broiling.

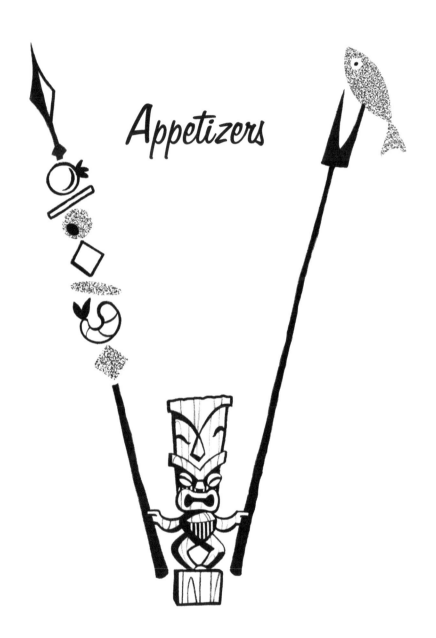

Appetizers

Illustration by Kevin Kidney

ALOHA SPREAD

12 ounces cream cheese, softened
2 ounces blue cheese, crumbled
1/3 cup fresh pineapple, finely chopped
1/3 cup chopped pecans, finely chopped
1/2 teaspoon ground ginger

Mix well and chill. Serve with Hawaiian lavosh
crackers.

Adapted by Mrs. Bum from a 1970 recipe of the same name.

CANLIS SHRIMP

2 tablespoons olive oil

2 tablespoons butter

2 pounds large shrimp, shelled and de-veined, leaving tails on

1/2 teaspoon salt

1/2 teaspoon fresh ground black pepper

1 ounce fresh lemon juice

2 ounces dry French vermouth

Blend olive oil and butter in large skillet over medium heat. Add shrimp, salt and pepper; cook shrimp till pink, up to 2 minutes. Add lemon juice and vermouth; continue cooking over high heat for one minute, stirring constantly. Serve hot. Serves 6 to 8.

As served at the Canlis Charcoal Broiler, Seattle, Washington, 1949. Owner Peter Canlis began cooking with vermouth during World War II, when wines were scarce. He continued the practice in his Waikiki Canlis Broiler, built in 1953 of redwood and moss lava, with an interior featuring a coral rock terrazzo, gas candelabra, mosaic murals, and a slant-roofed bar "lorded over by a friendly 12-foot Tiki enjoying the view and the visitors through pearl shell eyes." In both restaurants, up to six kimono-clad Japanese waitresses served each patron at a time.

CRAB RANGOON

1/2 pound Dungeness crab meat
1/2 pound cream cheese
dash A-1 sauce
dash garlic powder
1 egg yolk
salt to taste
white pepper to taste
puff paste mix

Prepare puff paste dough and roll extremely thin. Cut 4-by-4-inch squares. Clean crab meat well, chop and blend with other ingredients. Place 1 teaspoon of mixture in center of each square, moisten edges and fold. Deep fry until light brown and serve hot, with plum sauce and hot mustard (see page 96) on the side. Serves 4 to 5.

Pieces of eight

By Chef Paul Peron of the Pieces Of Eight restaurant, Marina Del Rey, California, circa 1965. Part of the Tallichet restaurant chain, which included the Ports O' Call in San Pedro and The Reef in Long Beach, Pieces Of Eight featured a panoramic view of the then-new Marina's yacht harbor. Patrons entered from a series of bridges, where they were met by a bewhiskered pirate with a live parrot on his shoulder. The interior carried through the buccaneer motif with muzzle-loading pistols, drapes cut from canvas sails, and a semi-private dining-room replica of a captain's quarters.

CURRY DIP

1 cup mayonnaise (Best Foods or Hellman's)
1 1/2 teaspoons curry powder
1/2 teaspoon dry (powdered) mustard
2 teaspoons lemon juice
1/8 teaspoon salt

Blend everything
together and chill.
Serve with crisp, raw
dipping vegetables.

From the Castaway restaurant, Burbank, California, circa 1960s. The island-themed Castaway chain had outposts throughout California, from San Bernadino to San Mateo. The Burbank restaurant is still open, but was gutted by fire around 20 years ago. It now suffers from a rather schizophrenic Country Charm-meets-South Of The Border makeover. If you can get past that, the hilltop view of the San Fernando Valley is worth the trip.

FLAMING HIBACHI BEEF

1 pound flank steak, trimmed of all fat, ends removed
1/2 cup soy sauce
1 tablespoon red wine
1 tablespoon curry powder
1 tablespoon sugar

To facilitate cutting, freeze steak overnight. Then cut into long thin strips (1/8" to 1/16" thick). Combine soy sauce, wine, curry and sugar. Marinate strips in the mixture for 30 minutes (no longer or soy sauce will obliterate other flavors), then thread each strip accordion-style onto its own bamboo skewer (see page 19). Arrange them in a pan and place under broiler just long enough to brown both sides. Transfer skewers to serving tray, bring to table with miniature preheated hibachi (pictured), and allow guests to finish cooking their beef over the hibachi's dramatically leaping sterno flame. Serves 6 to 12.

Circa 1960s.

FLAMING SHRIMP

1 pound medium-sized shrimp, shelled and de-veined, leaving tails on
1/4 cup butter
1/4 teaspoon salt
1/4 teaspoon pepper
1/2 cup dark Jamaican rum

Pre-warm rum in double-boiler. Sauté shrimp in butter until pink. Stir in salt and pepper. Turn into pre-heated chafing dish (or iron, non-Teflon-coated deep skillet, warmed but not too hot) with pre-warmed rum in bottom. Ignite rum from safe distance with long-stemmed match. Shake pan, and let flame burn down. Serve at once, with cocktail picks. Serves 4.

Circa 1962.

FRESH SALMON PURÉE, POLYNESIAN STYLE

1 pound fresh raw salmon, skin and bone removed
Juice of 2 large limes
2 tablespoons dry white wine
1 tablespoon aquavit
1 medium-sized onion, grated
1/4 cup mayonnaise (Best Foods or Hellman's)
2 teaspoons horseradish
1 tablespoon fresh dill, minced
2 teaspoons sugar
Salt, pepper, celery salt

Dice salmon very fine. Add all other ingredients -- *except* salt, pepper, and celery salt -- and mix thoroughly. Chill overnight in fridge. Before serving, add 1/2 teaspoon salt, 1/8 teaspoon pepper, and 1/8 teaspoon celery salt. Season with additional salt and pepper to taste.

Circa 1965. What makes this "Polynesian Style" is its passing resemblance to Lomi Lomi Salmon, a Hawaiian mélange of tomato, onion and smoked fish.

GINGER CHICKEN WINGS

2 pounds chicken wings, disjointed at first large bone

1 inch ginger root, sliced very thin

1/2 stick of butter

1/4 cup white wine

3/4 cup Shoyu (Japanese soy sauce)

1/4 cup sugar

3/4 cup water

Sauté sliced ginger in butter until transparent. Add chicken wings and fry until skin color changes. Add wine and cover tightly for a few seconds, until wine permeates chicken. Uncover and add shoyu, sugar, and water. Simmer 30-45 minutes, stirring often, until sauce has reduced and coated wings with a thick glaze. Serve with hot towels for finger-wiping. Serves 4 to 8.

Mrs. Hawaii**

A recipe entered in the 1963 Mrs. America contest by Laurie Bachran, winner of Mrs. Hawaii 1963. She was also the winner of that year's Mrs. Congeniality Award, the Snacks For Unexpected Guests Award, and (our favorite) Runner-up to Mrs. U.S. Savings Bonds.

LANGOUSTINE MIMOSA

1/2 pound softened butter
3/4 cup fine bread crumbs
1/2 clove garlic, minced very fine
1/2 tablespoon chopped shallots
1/2 tablespoon MSG (optional)
1/2 tablespoon chopped parsley
Dash Worcestershire sauce
Dash Tabasco
25 langoustines
3/4 cup dry white wine

Cream together softened butter, bread crumbs, garlic, shallots, MSG, parsley, Worcestershire and Tabasco, then set aside. In a skillet melt 2 tablespoons butter (*not* the set-aside special butter mix). Lightly sauté the langoustines in the butter. Add the wine and cook until wine is reduced by half. Place langoustines and wine sauce in shallow baking dish. Dot langoustines with the special butter mix (about 1 teaspoon per langoustine). Pre-heat oven to 425 degrees F. Bake in the hot oven for 4 minutes, or until butter has browned a bit. Sprinkle a little more fresh parsley on the langoustines just before serving.

By Trader Vic, 1961.

LUAU SWEET & SOUR SPARERIBS

3 pounds spareribs
Water
Salt
1/4 cup ketchup
1/2 cup white vinegar
2/3 cup plus 2 tablespoons sugar
6 drops hot pepper sauce (or to taste)

Simmer spareribs in salted water for 20 to 30 minutes. Drain and place in baking pan. Combine ketchup, vinegar, sugar, and pepper sauce with 1 cup water. Pour mixture over ribs, saving extra sauce, and bake at 350 degrees F. for 1 hour, basting every 10 minutes with extra sauce until ribs are richly browned and sticky. Serves 4.

BEVERLY HILLS

From the Luau restaurant, Beverly Hills, California (see *Intoxica*, page 53), circa 1959. The Luau was where other Polynesian restaurant chefs went to eat and tiki-bartenders to drink. Its celebrity clientele (movie Tarzan Gordon Scott and Beverly Hillbilly Max Baer, Jr., were among the many patrons caught diving naked into the lagoon) cemented its presence as one of L.A.'s "big three" exotic restaurants, alongside Don The Beachcomber's and Trader Vic's.

NATIVE DRUMS

30 chicken drumettes
1 cup soy sauce
1 cup brown sugar
1/2 cup butter
1 teaspoon dry (powdered) mustard
3/4 cup water

Place drumettes in shallow baking pan. Combine all other ingredients and heat until sugar and butter dissolve. Cool, then pour over drumettes. Marinate in fridge for 2 hours, turning occasionally. Bake in same pan, in marinade, for 45 minutes at 350 degrees F., turning once, and spooning marinade over chicken occasionally. Drain on paper towels.

Adapted from Chicken Wings Pacifica, a 1979 recipe by TV actress Betty White ("The Mary Tyler Moore Show") and game-show host Alan Ludden ("Password").

POISSON CRU

1 pound fresh raw white-fleshed fish (swordfish or mahimahi work well; scallops too)
1 teaspoon coarse salt (Kosher)
Juice of 6 limes
2 tablespoons chopped scallions
1 clove garlic, minced
1 cup coconut milk (see page 18)

Cut fish into bite-sized pieces. Sprinkle with salt and cover with lime juice. Cover and refrigerate for at least 4 hours. Drain lime juice. Add garlic and scallions to fish and mix well. Add coconut milk. Chill till serving time. (Individual serving suggestion: in large clam or scallop shells, placed on a bed of rock salt.) Serves 6 to 8.

TAHITI

A kind of South Seas ceviche, this traditional Tahitian raw fish dish is perhaps the only "real" Polynesian food that found its way onto Stateside menus. Circa 1930s.

ROAST TENDERLOIN OF PORK

1/2 cup sugar
1 1/2 teaspoons salt
1/8 teaspoon garlic powder
1/8 teaspoon white pepper
1/4 cup ketchup
1/4 cup soy sauce
1 tablespoon brandy
2 pork tenderloins, about 1/2 pound each
Hot mustard (see page 96)
sesame seeds (optional)

DON THE BEACHCOMBER®

Mix together first 6 ingredients. Stir in brandy. Marinate meat in mixture for 3 hours, turning occasionally. Line a shallow pan with foil and place drained tenderloins side by side in it. Roast at 400 degrees F. for 20 minutes. Turn pork, brush with marinade, and roast another 20 minutes. Brush

generously with marinade again and return to oven for about 5 minutes. Slice pork thin across the tenderloin, sprinkle with sesame seeds, and serve with hot mustard on the side. Serves 4.

By Don The Beachcomber, circa 1950s.

RUMAKI

12 large chicken livers
1 four-ounce can water chestnuts
12 slices bacon
1 cup soy sauce
1/2 cup sweet sherry
2 or 3 dashes hot pepper sauce
1 clove garlic, crushed
2 teaspoons finely sliced fresh ginger, or 1/2 teaspoon ground

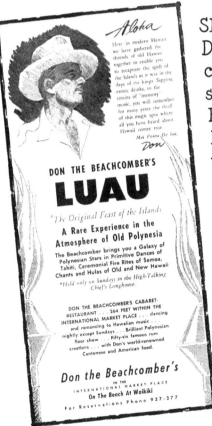

Slice chicken livers in half. Drain water chestnuts and cut into halves. Cut bacon slices in half, crosswise. Fold a piece of chicken liver around each piece of water chestnut; wrap with a half-slice of bacon and secure with a toothpick (see page 19).

Mix soy sauce, sherry, pepper sauce, garlic and ginger. Marinate rumaki in mixture for one hour minimum, or as long as overnight. Drain.

Broil under a range broiler until bacon is crisp, usually about 5 or 6 minutes, turning to cook evenly. Yields 24 Rumaki.

For the chicken liver phobic, try:

OYSTER RUMAKI

Strain 24 large whole canned oysters and soak them in a marinade of bottled teriyaki sauce mixed with crushed fresh garlic to taste (3 cloves maximum). Pre-fry 12 strips of bacon until pink and soft; drain on paper towels. Wrap half a strip of bacon around each whole oyster and a slice of water chestnut, secure each with a toothpick, and fry the lot until crispy.

The quintessential *faux*-Polynesian pupu, invented mid-century by Don The Beachcomber (see page 12 for origin myth). The oyster version is by Truus De Groot, a.k.a. Trader Dutch of the Tiki Objects By Bosko organization (see page 96). In addition to oysters, other restaurants later introduced many variations on the Rumaki theme, substituting shrimp, lobster, lychees, and even kumquats for the artery-jamming chicken livers. But since most of these recipes called for deep-fat frying instead of broiling, the cholesterol count probably wasn't that much lower.

SHRIMP LUAU

2 pounds large shrimp
Juice of 2 lemons
Curry powder
Powdered ginger
Salt
3 cups flour
3 teaspoons double-action baking powder
1 cup milk
2 cups shredded coconut (see page 18)

Shell, de-vein, and split shrimp lengthwise, leaving tails intact. Marinate shrimp for 4 hours in the lemon juice, seasoned with 1 teaspoon curry powder, a pinch of powdered ginger, and salt to taste.

Next, sift flour with baking powder and a pinch of salt. Beat in milk and the marinade drained from the shrimp to make a smooth batter. Spread shredded coconut in a shallow baking dish and toast it lightly in oven pre-heated to

350 degrees F., stirring frequently to assure even browning.

Dust the shrimp with flour, dip them in the batter, and roll them in the toasted coconut. Deep fry at 375 degrees F. to a rich golden brown and serve hot, with any of the usual sauces for fried shrimp, flavored with curry if desired. Serves 6 to 8.

Haoli Wela kahau!

FROM THE

Hawaiian Room

HOTEL LEXINGTON at 48th ST., NEW YORK CITY

2 SHOWS NIGHTLY
For Private Luaus
Call Banquet Dept.

RESERVATIONS:
PLaza 5-4400

As served in the Hawaiian Room at the Hotel Lexington, New York City, 1958, the year *New York Daily News* columnist Danton Walker wrote in his *Guide To New York Nightlife*: "The story of the Hawaiian Room dates from 1937. The management of the Lexington Hotel, completed six months before the market crash of 1929 and costing $5,000,000, found itself stuck with a large and useless basement dining room ... manager Charles Rochester decided to experiment for a few months with all-Hawaiian entertainment in a cafe decorated with South Seas motifs and featuring Polynesian food." The chefs were Swiss, but the acts were authentic; the show, starring a singing comedienne named Hilo Hattie, was an instant success, making the room as well known in Honolulu and San Francisco as in Manhattan. At the room's peak in the mid-1950s, Steve Allen and Arthur Godfrey both broadcast TV shows from there.

TIKI-TIKI CHICKEN IN PARCHMENT

1 pound raw white chicken meat
2 tablespoons gin
2 tablespoons hoisin sauce
2 tablespoons ketchup
1 tablespoon peanut oil
1 teaspoon salt
2 bunches scallions

Cut chicken into 1-inch squares, 1/4 inch thick. Put the pieces into a bowl and cover with gin, hoisin, ketchup, peanut oil, and salt. Let the chicken marinate for 2 to 3 hours.

Cut scallions into 1-inch lengths. Wrap 2 pieces of chicken and 2 of scallion in small squares of parchment or aluminum foil. Fold edges of the packages over to make a very tight seal (or else wrapper will open and spill out contents during cooking).

Deep fry at 380 degrees F. for 3 minutes and serve immediately. Serves 4.

As served at The Islander restaurant, Beverly Hills, California, 1962. This "Technicolor Polynesia" was one of the most expensive evenings on La Cienega Boulevard's restaurant row, but you got what you paid for: Rickshaw drivers ran you up a steep zigzag path through a lush tropical lagoon, to the grand entrance of a dizzyingly high-ceilinged, A-frame structure that seamlessly melded primitive architecture with sleek moderne design. Inside you experienced "a daring departure in fine dining," sampling "Comestibles Pacifica" and "the unique and strangely haunting beverages of this huge, island-dotted territory" in a multi-level interior of corrugated woods and aquariums stocked with exotic fish. The Islander was demolished in the 1970s; the site is now home to a particularly ugly Mexican restaurant.

Entrées

BEEF RIBS LUAU

2 cups Heinz ketchup
1/4 cup sugar
1/8 teaspoon minced garlic
1/4 cup Chinese barbecue sauce (char siu)
2 tablespoons dry white wine
16 to 20 beef back ribs (about 10 pounds)

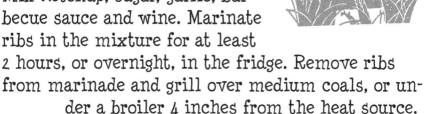

Mix ketchup, sugar, garlic, barbecue sauce and wine. Marinate ribs in the mixture for at least 2 hours, or overnight, in the fridge. Remove ribs from marinade and grill over medium coals, or under a broiler 4 inches from the heat source. Baste ribs often with marinade until they're browned, about 10 minutes a side. Serves 4.

Dine At ..
THE
LUAU
of Beverly Hills
Polynesian and American Cuisine
LUNCHEON • COCKTAILS • DINNER
421 N. Rodeo Dr., Beverly Hills, BR 2-8484

From the Luau restaurant, Beverly Hills, California (see page 30), circa 1966. Luau Maître d' Joe Stellini took this recipe with him when he left in 1975 to open his own Beverly Hills restaurant -- named, oddly enough, Stellini's. Even odder: The secret ingredient to the Luau's much sought-after rib recipe was ... Heinz ketchup.

CHICKEN OF THE GODS

2 1/2 to 3 pounds boned-and-skinned chicken
   breasts
1 egg, beaten
1/4 teaspoon salt
3 tablespoons sherry
1 tablespoon soy sauce
Dash white pepper
1/2 pound water chestnut flour (see page 96)
4 cups chicken stock (canned will do)
1/2 cube soft butter
2 tablespoons cornstarch
1 cup cream
Salt
Pepper
1/2 cup mushrooms, sliced
2 teaspoons browned sesame seeds

Cut chicken into thin, flat pieces, similar to filets
of sole. Marinate slices in beaten egg, salt, sherry,
soy sauce and white pepper for 30 minutes. Cover

each piece of chicken with water chestnut flour. Fry in deep oil at 350 degrees F. until golden brown.

Melt butter over medium heat and blend in cornstarch. Bring stock to boil and stir rapidly while adding butter mixture. Reduce heat and add cream, seasonings and mushrooms.

Cut chicken pieces into neat, finger-length slices and arrange on hot platter. Cover with cream sauce and sprinkle with sesame seeds. Serve with rice. Serves 4 to 6.

By Chef "Bobby" SooHoo of the Bali Hai restaurant, San Diego, California (see *Intoxica*, page 15), circa 1957. When Hawaiian restaurateur Sam Choy took over the Bali Hai in the 1990s, he replaced every item on the menu with his own dishes. Nobody complained -- except when it came to Chicken Of The Gods, which long-time regulars requested so often that Choy eventually restored it to the menu.

COCONUT DUCKLING

3 14-ounce cans coconut milk (see page 18)

1 five pound, ready-to-cook duckling

butter

2 pineapples, leafy stems attached

1 papaya

1 cup shredded coconut (see page 18)

2 cloves garlic, minced

2 onions, chopped

2 inch piece of fresh ginger root, peeled and chopped

1 tablespoon curry powder

5 tablespoons flour

salt

Chill 2 unopened cans of coconut milk overnight, or until milk congeals into coconut cream (see page 18 for details).

HOTEL

Hana-Maui

HAWAIIAN ISLANDS

Cut the 2 leg and thigh pieces, and each side of the breast from duckling. Trim the pieces of all excess fat. In a large skillet, heat 4 tablespoons butter and sauté duckling pieces until lightly browned on both sides. Add 1 cup water, cover, and simmer for 1 hour or until tender. While duck is simmering:

Toast shredded coconut and set aside.

Halve pineapples lengthwise up through leafy stems (which should remain attached to enhance the final dramatic presentation). Carefully remove pineapple meat, leaving a shell about 1/2 inch thick. Discard

hard core of meat and dice the rest.
Set diced pineapple and shells aside.
Peel one small papaya. Discard
seeds and slice meat. Set aside.

Pre-heat oven to 350 degrees F.

In a saucepan, melt 2 tablespoons butter. Add garlic,
onion, and ginger and cook for about 20 minutes, or
until onion is tender and golden. Stir in curry powder and cook, stirring, for one minute. Stir in flour.
Open your third, unchilled can of coconut milk and
stir 1 1/2 cups of it into the curry mixture. Add salt
to taste and cook over low heat for 15 minutes, stirring occasionally. Pour mixture from saucepan into
electric blender. Blend on high speed for 15 seconds.
Pour back into saucepan and stir in 2 1/2 cups of
your congealed coconut cream. Heat, but do not let
boil or coconut cream will curdle.

In each half-pineapple shell, put a layer of sliced papaya and top with a layer of diced pineapple. Cover
with 2 tablespoons of curry sauce and heat in 350-
degree oven for 15 minutes. Place slices of duck in
each pineapple shell and cover with curry sauce.
Sprinkle with the toasted coconut and serve each
guest his or her own individual shell. Serves 4.

Merely one of 26 courses served during the luau at the Hotel Hana-Maui,
Hawaii, 1964 -- not counting the *piece de resistance* of whole pig roasted
with hot stones in an underground fire-pit. As frequent Hana-Maui
guest Vincent Price once observed of preparing a proper luau: "It can't
all be achieved with a can of pineapple and a dash of soy sauce."

DOUBLE FRUIT-GLAZED PORK CHOPS

6 6-to-8-ounce double-rib pork chops
Salt
Pepper
2 cups brown sugar
1/2 cup unsweetened pineapple juice
1/2 cup honey
2 teaspoons dry (powdered) mustard
6 whole cloves
12 whole coriander seeds, crushed

Brown chops in skillet; season with salt and pepper, then place in shallow baking pan. Combine remaining ingredients for sauce, and spoon about 3 tablespoons over each chop. Bake uncovered at 350 degrees F. till done (up to 1 hour), basting now and then with rest of sauce.

With toothpick, peg a slice each of orange, lemon, and lime on every chop, top-

on the water's edge

Kona Inn

WAIAKA WING
Kona Coast, Hawaii

INTER-ISLAND RESORTS
307 Lewers St.
936 511
ALSO KAUAI INN, NANILOA.

ping pick with maraschino cherry; baste fruit with sauce and bake 10 minutes longer.

Serves 6. To serve, arrange chops on leaf-lined platter with orchids and Honeyed Bananas:

HONEYED BANANAS

Peel 6 bananas; dip in lemon juice. Melt 2 tablespoons butter in skillet; stir in 1/4 cup honey. Add bananas, cook over low heat, turning gently, until hot and glazed. Don't overcook -- takes only a few minutes.

By Lee Siebenthaler, Executive Chef of the Kona Inn, Kailua-Kona, Hawaii, 1964. Then part of the Inter-Island Resort chain, which included the Kauai Surf and the Naniloa in Hilo, the Kona Inn featured rather avant-garde oil paintings of abstract tiki faces in every room, as well as modernist mosaics of local deep-sea fish (marlin fishing was the chief attraction for many of the inn's guests). In addition to four restaurants, the Inn also boasted a bamboo pipe organ and early 19th-century nautical artifacts in its Whaler's Bar.

FONDUE POLYNÉSIENNE

3 pounds sirloin steak, chicken, or shrimp (or a combination of all three)
1 cup soy sauce
1/3 cup brown sugar
2 tablespoons sherry
2 cloves garlic, minced
2 slices fresh ginger root, minced
1 scallion, chopped fine
Dash of fresh pepper
3 cups peanut oil for fondue pot

Cut steak or chicken into 1-inch cubes. Shrimp should be left whole, cleaned and de-veined. Combine soy sauce, sugar, sherry, garlic, ginger, scallion and pepper. Pour the mixture over beef, chicken or shrimp. Toss and turn to coat well.

Marinate overnight in fridge, or 3-4 hours at room temp. Drain and arrange on platter over beds of parsley or watercress.

Fill fondue pot 1/2 full of oil (more and you risk bubbling over when meat is cooked). Heat to about 375 degrees F. Test oil with a bread cube; if it cooks brown and crisp in 30 seconds or so, oil is hot enough for fonduing. Adjust burner so that oil will remain at burning point throughout meal.

Each guest spears a cube of meat, chicken or whole shrimp with a long-handled fondue skewer and dunks it into the hot oil, cooking to taste (10 seconds for rare up to a minute for well done). Serves 6.

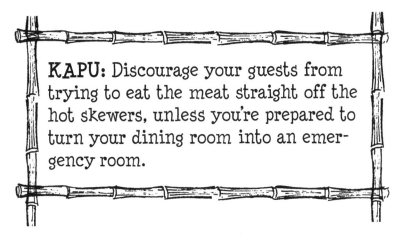

KAPU: Discourage your guests from trying to eat the meat straight off the hot skewers, unless you're prepared to turn your dining room into an emergency room.

From the Hawaii Kai, New York City (see *Grog Log*, pages 39 and 41), circa 1960s, when the restaurant's bamboo huts and lava-rock gardens were, according to management, "jealously guarded by Tiki Gods." This dish is ideal for island-themed dinner parties, considering it's the closest most of us will ever come to boiling missionaries in a pot. (A notion that would have displeased the Hawaii Kai's devout, hymn-spouting doorman, an African-American midget named Pee Wee who kept Broadway's riffraff out of the restaurant for two decades. According to Josh Alan Friedman in his book *Tales Of Times Square*, the four-foot-eight Pee Wee dressed "in an old-fashioned blue-and-gray doorman's uniform that he 'messes up' with a rose in his lapel, a police button, an American flag, two religious emblems, a diamond stickpin under his bowtie, and gold jewelry, making him look like a tiny, decorated general.")

JAVANESE LAMB SATÉ

2 pounds lamb leg, boneless and butterflied
2/3 cup canola oil
2 teaspoons ground coriander
2 teaspoons ground cumin
4 whole cloves
2-inch stick of cinnamon, broken into pieces
2 teaspoons fresh ginger, finely minced
1 teaspoon garlic, chopped
1 teaspoon salt
1 teaspoon crushed dried red pepper

Cut lamb into cubes app. 1-inch thick and set aside. Pour all other ingredients into blender. Blend at high speed for about 2 minutes, or until whole spices are coarsely ground. Pour over lamb in mixing bowl. Marinate overnight. Fasten meat on skewers (see page 19). Broil under pre-heated broiler flame until brown. Serves 4. Serve with saté sauce on the side:

SATÉ SAUCE

Sauté 3 tablespoons finely minced onion and 1/2 teaspoon finely minced garlic in oil until onion is lightly browned. Turn into saucepan, adding 1 tablespoon fresh lemon juice, 1 cup coconut milk (see page 18), and 1/4 cup peanut butter. Simmer until sauce is smooth and hot, stirring constantly. Season with salt and pepper to taste.

Circa 1965.

MAHIMAHI REEF HOTEL

2 eggs
dry white wine
lemon juice
salt
pepper
6 mahimahi filets, 1 inch thick
flour
butter
2 chervil leaves, finely chopped (or 1/2 tsp. dried chervil)
 1 1/2 cups macadamia nuts, finely chopped

THE *Reef* HOTEL

Beat eggs and add 1/3 cup dry white wine and 1 tablespoon lemon juice. Salt and pepper fish filets to taste. Dip filets in the egg mixture and dredge them in flour. Sauté filets in 1/4 cup butter, turning once, until done. Sprinkle chervil over filets just prior to removing from heat. Heat macadamia nuts in 2 tablespoons butter, adding 2/3 cup dry white wine and 1 tablespoon lemon juice. When nuts are heated through, pour the nuts and wine over the fish. Serves 6.

As served at the Chief's Hut in the Reef Hotel, Waikiki, Hawaii, 1960.

MALAYAN STEAK

1 1/2 pounds sirloin steak
2 tablespoons olive oil
6 scallions, cut in 1-inch lengths
1/4 cup Chinese oyster sauce (see page 96)
1 tablespoon cornstarch
1/4 cup water

Slice beef very thin and trim all fat. Sauté beef in the hot oil, no more than 30 seconds on each side. Add scallions and oyster sauce. Cook over low heat up to 4 minutes. Mix the cornstarch and water and add to the steak, stirring steadily until thickened. Serve with rice. Serves 3.

From the Luau restaurant, Atlanta, Georgia, 1960. The Atlanta Luau (not affiliated with the Beverly Hills Luau of pages 30 and 41) housed five dining rooms, each decorated in the style of a different island: Tahiti, Fiji, Samoa, Oahu, and the big island of Hawaii. The building itself was in the sleek "primitive-moderne" style, fronted by an imposing conical *porte-cochere*.

Montea Kristo
Ai - Mama

6 slices each cooked turkey, cooked ham, Swiss cheese	1/4 teaspoon salt
	1 1/3 cups water
	1 egg
12 slices white bread	Oil for deep frying
1 1/2 cups flour	Powdered sugar
1 tablespoon baking powder	Passion fruit preserves or guava jelly

Make 6 sandwiches, each with 1 slice turkey, 1 slice cheese, and 1 slice ham (in that order). Cut each sandwich into quarters, holding each quarter together with a wood pick.

THE FABULOUS

Tahitian Terrace

IN ADVENTURELAND

Sift flour, baking powder, and salt. Add water to beaten egg and mix with sifted flour into a batter. Dip each sandwich quarter into batter and fry in heated oil to 360 degrees F. until golden brown. Remove picks, sprinkle with powdered sugar, and serve with jelly on the side. Serves 6.

From the Tahitian Terrace restaurant, Disneyland, 1962. Known outside "the wondrous realm of Polynesia" as a Monte Cristo sandwich (see page 14), this dish was served to diners under a 35-foot-tall artificial tree with 14,075 hand-grafted leaves ("species Disneydendron"). The Tahitian Terrace closed in 1993 to make way for Aladdin's Oasis.

PEA PODS AND WATER CHESTNUTS

2 tablespoons peanut oil
1/2 pound lean pork, cut into 1/8-inch strips
8 ounces water chestnuts, drained and sliced
4 ounces sliced mushrooms
1/4 cup thinly sliced bamboo shoots
1/4 cup thinly sliced celery
10 1/2 ounces condensed chicken broth
1 pound Chinese pea pods, stringed and washed
1 clove garlic, crushed
2 tablespoons soy sauce
dash cayenne
2 tablespoons cornstarch
1/4 cup water

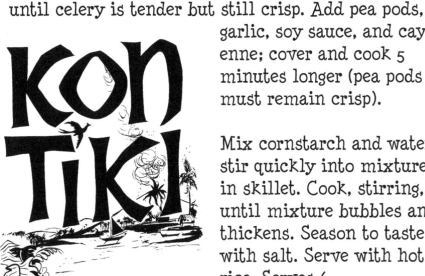

In a large skillet heat oil just until it starts to smoke. Add pork and stir quickly over high heat until almost cooked, up to 2 minutes. Add water chestnuts, mushrooms, bamboo shoots, celery, and chicken broth. Stir to blend, lower heat and cover. Cook until celery is tender but still crisp. Add pea pods, garlic, soy sauce, and cayenne; cover and cook 5 minutes longer (pea pods must remain crisp).

Mix cornstarch and water; stir quickly into mixture in skillet. Cook, stirring, until mixture bubbles and thickens. Season to taste with salt. Serve with hot rice. Serves 6.

By Chef Bing Ben Chan of the Kon-Tiki restaurant, Cleveland, Ohio, circa 1960s. Part of Steven Crane's nationwide Kon-Tiki chain (see *Intoxica*, page 81), this outpost promised "unfamiliar delights to the armchair -- or the dinner-table -- traveler" who was willing to trade "the everyday world of Cleveland for the exotic fare and island decor of Polynesia. A pool, a waterfall, a profusion of plants set the scene; the walls are decorated with tapa cloths, carvings, ancient weapons, shields, and Tiki gods."

SHELLFISH POLYNESIAN

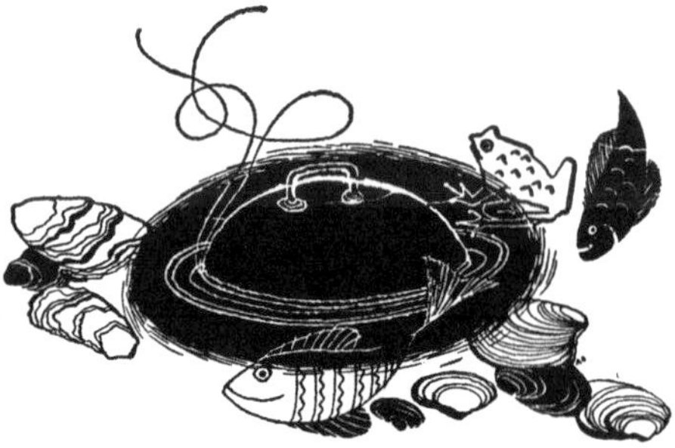

30 good-sized scallops
1 cup soy sauce
2/3 cup dry red wine
1/4 cup sherry
1/2 cup pineapple juice
1/2 cup brown sugar
1/4 cup melted butter
1/4 teaspoon dry (powdered) mustard
1/4 teaspoon thyme
1 teaspoon ground ginger
1 teaspoon Worcestershire sauce
30 medium shrimp, cooked and cleaned

Cover scallops with water; bring to a boil, drain, and set aside. In a bowl, combine soy sauce, red wine, sherry, pineapple juice, sugar, butter, mustard, thyme, ginger and Worcestershire sauce. Marinate the scallops and shrimp in the mixture for 2 hours. Alternate shrimp and scallops on skewers (see page 19). Broil 3 minutes on each side. Serve with rice and sautéed pineapple slices. Serves 6-10.

From the Lahala House restaurant, Corpus Christi, Texas, 1959.

SHRIMP CHOW DUN

1 tablespoon sesame oil
1/2 teaspoon salt
1 teaspoon MSG (optional)
1/2 pound shrimp
1 ounce mushrooms, sliced
1 ounce onion, sliced
1 ounce water chestnuts, chopped finely
1 ounce fresh green peas
3 eggs

Place oil, salt and MSG in wok. Add shrimp and cook with mushrooms, onion, water chestnuts, and peas till shrimp turns pink. Add slightly beaten eggs and serve. Serves 2.

DON THE BEACHCOMBER
PALM SPRINGS, CALIFORNIA

As served at Don The Beachcomber's, circa 1940s.

STEAK KEW

3 pounds top-grade sirloin, trimmed of all fat
1/4 cup butter, melted
1 teaspoon soy sauce
1/2 cup Chinese oyster sauce (see page 96)
1 teaspoon sugar
1/2 cup water chestnuts, sliced
1/2 cup mushrooms, sliced
1/2 cup bamboo shoots
1 cup Chinese pea pods
1/2 cup cornstarch
1/2 cup sherry

Cut sirloin into 1-inch cubes. In a deep skillet combine the beef, butter, soy and oyster sauce. Cover and sauté for 1 to 2 minutes. Remove beef from the pan, add vegetables to the beef stock, and cook uncovered over low flame for 2 minutes, stirring in cornstarch and sherry. Replace beef and cook 2 more minutes, stirring constantly. Serves 6.

From Bali Ha'i At The Beach, New Orleans, Louisiana, 1967. Owner Harry J. Batt, Sr., decorated the longhouse dining room with souvenirs from his Pacific excursions. Said Batt of his collection: "The Tiki Gods, the native beauty of Samoan tapa cloth, woven palm fronds from Hawaii, native spears from Taiwan and vari-colored Japanese fish floats and Shigi fish traps combine to form a new world of South Sea Enchantment."

TERIYAKI STEAK

2 cloves garlic, crushed
6 ounces soy sauce
1/2 cup brown sugar
2 tablespoons grated fresh ginger root
1 tablespoon Sake
2 rib-eye steaks

Mix first 5 ingredients into a sauce and let stand for an hour or two. Then marinate steaks in sauce for 30 minutes to one hour (no longer or saltiness of soy sauce will take over). Broil to taste. Thoroughly heat the extra sauce and serve on the side. Serves 2.

From the Kalua Room, Seattle, Washington, 1955. After a stint operating restaurants in Hawaii, Gwynne Austin opened the Kalua Room in the upscale Windsor Hotel. Two ring-tailed monkeys greeted arriving customers from inside a plate-glass, air-conditioned cage. Waitresses wore skimpy "native" costumes, distracting diners from such other sights as a lagoon with floating orchids and hanging stalks of real bananas.

2   WASH. ATHLETIC CLUB
3   FREDERICK & NELSON
4   I. MAGNIN CO.
5   LITTLER'S
6   BON MARCHE
7   BEST'S
        T - THEATRES

Tapa Room
AVAILABLE FOR
PRIVATE PARTIES

TRADE WINDS CURRIED SHRIMP

1/2 pound shrimp, shelled and de-veined
1 tablespoon flour
1/2 teaspoon salt
1 cup milk or light cream
1 tablespoon curry
1 tablespoon onion, finely minced
Butter

Melt 1 tablespoon butter in small saucepan; over low heat blend in flour and salt. Gradually add the milk, stirring steadily to the boiling point. Cook over low heat for 5 minutes, then fold in curry and set aside.

Sauté the shrimp and onion in butter. Then add the cream sauce and remove from the fire. Serve over rice. Serves 2.

From the Trade Winds restaurant, Chicago, Illinois, 1944. Owner Hy Ginnis's night spot, "where every customer is Mr. Trade Winds," was an after-hours hangout for touring comedians like Jimmy Durante, Joe E. Lewis, and Milton Berle.

Soup, Salads & Sides

Illustration by Kevin Kidney

BONGO BONGO SOUP

10 ounces fresh oysters, poached (or 10 ounces drained, canned oysters)

1/4 cup strained Gerber's Baby Food spinach

2 1/2 cups half-and-half

2 tablespoons butter

1 teaspoon MSG (optional)

1 teaspoon A-1 sauce

1/2 teaspoon salt

About 3/8 teaspoon freshly ground black pepper

Generous dash garlic salt

Generous dash cayenne

2 teaspoons cornstarch mixed with 2 teaspoons cold water

About 2/3 cup heavy cream, whipped (see page 19)

Puree oysters in a blender. In a large saucepan, heat half-and-half just to simmering. Add oyster puree, spinach, butter, MSG, A-1 sauce, salt, pepper, garlic salt, and cayenne. Heat to simmering, whisking until smooth; do not boil. Add cornstarch mixture, then heat and stir with a whisk until soup is slightly thickened.

Ladle into heatproof serving bowls. Top each with spoonful of whipped cream. Slip under broiler just until cream is well glazed and slightly brown. Serves 4.

By Trader Vic, who dished about his soup in a 1973 autobiography: "When we first made it, we used Toheroa clams from New Zealand. This is a peculiar kind of clam and only the Maori natives are allowed to harvest them. During the war we had an outfit that canned them with a phony label so they could be shipped out of the country. The Toheroa clam lives on a green algae which gave the soup its green color. That's why in the current recipe I use baby spinach." Above version circa 1950s.

FRIED RICE A LA KONA

4 cups boiled rice, chilled*

1 tablespoon chopped green onions

1 tablespoon chopped Canadian bacon

1 scrambled egg

2 tablespoons soy sauce

1 tablespoon peanut oil

1 teaspoon fresh ginger root, chopped fine

Kona Kai Club
450 YACHT HARBOR DRIVE
SAN DIEGO CALIFORNIA

In a heavy skillet, heat peanut oil and add green onions and Canadian bacon, followed by cold boiled rice (*warm rice will result in a sticky mess). Fry rice until dry, then add soy sauce, ginger root and egg. Sauté well and serve hot. Serves 4.

By Chef Felix De Sano of the Kona Kai Club and Kona Inn, San Diego, California, 1962. The Kona Kai was a private club, while the Kona Inn was open to the public. The Inn's nautical-themed Voyager Room overlooked the yacht basin of San Diego's Shelter Island.

PAKE NOODLES

1 cup hot cooked noodles (udon or lo mein work well)

3 tablespoons butter

2 tablespoons sesame seeds, toasted

1 tablespoon fine dry bread crumbs

1/4 teaspoon MSG (optional)

salt

black pepper

Mix together hot noodles, butter, bread crumbs, sesame seeds and MSG. Season to taste with salt and pepper. Serves 1 or 2.

As served at Trader Vic's in the Savoy Hilton, New York City, 1959. Perhaps because of its spectacular art direction -- the combined effort of no less than 10 design firms -- the New York Trader Vic's was a favorite haunt of film producer Darryl F. Zanuck and directors Bob Fosse and Stanley Kubrick. Salvador Dali was also a fan. "Pake" is Hawaiian for "Chinese."

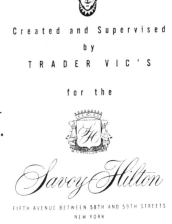

Created and Supervised
by
T R A D E R   V I C ' S

for the

Savoy Hilton

FIFTH AVENUE BETWEEN 58TH AND 59TH STREETS
NEW YORK

PITCAIRN SALAD

1 cup mayonnaise

1/4 cup Roquefort cheese

1/4 cup apple cider vinegar

1 tablespoon white Worcestershire sauce

2 tablespoons scallions, chopped very fine

1 teaspoon sugar

Salad greens (iceberg or butter lettuce)

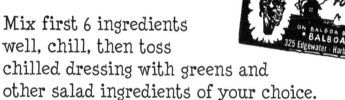

Mix first 6 ingredients well, chill, then toss chilled dressing with greens and other salad ingredients of your choice.

Mrs. Bum updated this 1954 recipe from Christian's Hut, Balboa Bay, California. Named after Fletcher Christian -- who in 1789 led the Bounty mutineers to Pitcairn Island -- Christian's Hut was opened in the late 1930s by Art La Shelle, brother of Oscar-winning cinematographer Joseph La Shelle. In addition to patrons Red Skelton, Fred MacMurray and Howard Hughes, the restaurant boasted its own dock for diners arriving by sea. It also boasted "The Goof," a giant, ghoulish head wearing a top hat and an evil grin from its rooftop perch. Over the years, The Goof mysteriously migrated south to San Diego's Shelter Island, where he is now grinning from the top of the Bali Hai (see pages 42-43). Christian's Hut burned down in 1963; the Newport Towers now occupy the site.

STUFFED LOBSTER SALAD

5 cooked lobster tails
2 stalks celery, chopped
1/4 teaspoon salt
Pinch of pepper
Juice of 1 lemon
1/2 cup mayonnaise

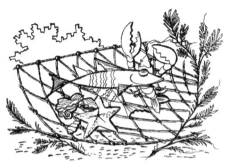

Remove lobster meat from shells (saving shells) and cut into bite-size pieces. Combine remaining ingredients -- *except* mayonnaise -- and mix well. Add mayonnaise a little at a time until you have desired consistency. Place salad mixture back in shells and serve on bed of lettuce garnished with lemon wedges. Serves 5.

From La Ronde restaurant, Honolulu, Hawaii, 1961, when La Ronde was touted as the first revolving restaurant in America atop the tallest building in Hawaii located in the largest shopping center in the world. Powered by three 3-horsepower electric motors, the flying saucer-shaped dining room completed one full rotation an hour, at a speed of 3 feet per minute.

SWEET POTATOES AU RHUM

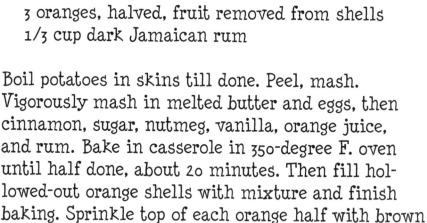

2 pounds sweet potatoes, washed
1/2 cup butter, melted
3 eggs, slightly beaten
1 teaspoon cinnamon
3/4 cup brown sugar
1/2 cup granulated sugar
1 teaspoon nutmeg
1 teaspoon vanilla extract
1 cup orange juice
3 oranges, halved, fruit removed from shells
1/3 cup dark Jamaican rum

Boil potatoes in skins till done. Peel, mash. Vigorously mash in melted butter and eggs, then cinnamon, sugar, nutmeg, vanilla, orange juice, and rum. Bake in casserole in 350-degree F. oven until half done, about 20 minutes. Then fill hollowed-out orange shells with mixture and finish baking. Sprinkle top of each orange half with brown sugar and let brown lightly, till sugar's caramelized. Serves 6.

The Polynesians cultivated sweet potatoes centuries before European contact -- but since the tuber is native only to the Andes, nobody knows how the Polynesians got ahold of it. In the 1950s Thor Heyerdahl used the mystery to support his contention that South Americans colonized the Pacific, a theory historians have since dropped like, well, a hot potato.

Desserts

BANANA CALYPSO FLAMBÉ

1 ounce unsalted butter
2 bananas, halved cross-
wise, then lengthwise
2 tablespoons brown
sugar
Juice of 1 lime
1 teaspoon ground ginger
3 ounces rum
2 scoops vanilla ice
cream

Pre-heat rum in double-
boiler. Heat skillet, add butter, and place the bananas in
the pan. Sauté slightly. Add
brown sugar, lime juice, and
ginger. Stir well until sauce
turns into a thick molas-
ses. Add the rum and, from
a safe distance, flambé with
long-stem match (see page
19). Dish up the ice cream

NEXT BEST THING TO YOUR OWN ISLAND

ISLANDIA
hotel · restaurant

on two plates, placing the bananas on top of the ice
cream. Serve at once. Serves 2.

From the Islandia restaurant, San Diego, California, 1961.

CHERRIES HAWAIIANA

1 pound can of Bing cherries
1 teaspoon Curacao liqueur
1 teaspoon cornstarch
Myers' dark Jamaican rum
Coconut ice cream

Drain cherries, saving the syrup. Combine 1/4 cup of syrup with Curacao and 1/2 cup rum. Marinate cherries in this mixture for 3 hours. Then make a paste out of cornstarch and a little syrup; add to fruit mixture. Bring to a simmer for 1 minute in blazer pan of chafing dish, or in metal saucepan.

Fill a ladle with rum, lower ladle in heated fruit mixture to warm rum, then ignite rum from safe distance with long-stemmed match. Pour flaming rum over fruit mixture, setting mixture aflame. Let flame burn a while before extinguishing; spoon cherries over individual servings of ice cream. Serves 6.

A 1960 recipe by the Myers' Rum Company.

HUK-AI-PIE

14 crisp gingersnaps
5 tablespoons melted butter
1 1/4 cups milk
2 eggs, well beaten
1/2 cup sugar
3 2/3 tablespoons cornstarch
1 ounce Baker's bitter chocolate, melted
1 teaspoon vanilla
1 tablespoon light rum
3/4 cup whipping cream
1/2 ounce bitter chocolate, broken into tiny chips

Make gingersnap crust by rolling the crisp gingersnaps out fine, then adding 5 tablespoons melted butter. Pat evenly into 9-inch pie tin and bake 10 minutes at 300 degrees F. Set aside to cool.

Scald milk in double boiler, then whisk in beaten eggs (very slowly, or they'll

scramble) and blend well. Mix sugar and cornstarch and stir into egg mixture.

Cook 15-20 minutes in double boiler, stirring occasionally. When cooked custard generously coats spoon, it's done. Take 1/3 of hot custard and mix slowly with melted chocolate until cool. Add vanilla to chocolate custard.

Stir remaining 2/3 of custard slowly until cool to avoid lumping. When cool, add rum and blend.

Whip cream until it peaks (see page 19 for instructions).

Dobbs House
LUAU

Add chocolate filling to cooled gingersnap crust, completely covering crust. Add rum custard and level across pie. Top with whipped cream and sprinkle with chips of chocolate. Serves 8.

From the Dobbs House Luau restaurant chain, which stretched across the South in the late 1950s. There were Dobbs Houses in Atlanta, Georgia; Birmingham, Alabama; Charlotte, North Carolina; Memphis, Tennessee; Dallas and Houston, Texas; Lexington and Louisville, Kentucky; and Miami and Orlando, Florida. This recipe, "A sorcerer's blend of rich dark chocolate and rum," hails from the Memphis restaurant, which featured a 25-foot Easter Island head and a pool of water from which a flame erupted; in addition to an "exotic menu" allegedly "the end product of years of research," they also served "many old Southern favorites."

KONA COFFEE SABAYON

6 egg yolks
1 cup sugar
1 tablespoon vanilla
sugar (see page 96)
Grated rind of 1/4 orange
1 cup double strength Kona coffee
1/4 cup Kona coffee liqueur

Beat yolks, sugars and rind until very light. Cook this mixture in a double-boiler, whipping it constantly with a wire whisk until foamy. Gradually add coffee and liqueur and continue whipping constantly and vigorously until mixture becomes frothy and stiff (this could take as long as 6 minutes). Serve immediately in pre-warmed champagne glasses, with a light cookie (such as ladyfingers). Serves 6.

From the Kona Village, Kaupulehu, Hawaii, circa 1960s. Built around the beach and ponds of an ancient fishing village on the Big Island's rocky Kona coast, this upscale resort provided an escape into the primitive world for those from the modern world who could afford it. The individual thatched huts offered maximum seclusion, with no TV or radio inside, but the food and service had (and still have) one of the best reputations in the islands.

MAI TAI PIE

1 envelope unflavored gelatin

3 eggs, separated

2/3 cup granulated sugar, divided

1/4 teaspoon salt

Mai Tai mix (1 ounce fresh lime juice, 1/2 ounce orange curacao, 1/4 ounce each orgeat and rock candy syrups)

1 teaspoon grated lemon rind

1 ounce light rum

1/2 ounce dark Jamaican rum

1 baked 9-inch pie crust, cooled

1/2 cup Beachbum's Rum Whipped Cream (see page 19)

Soften gelatin in 1/4 cup water. Beat egg yolks; stir in 1/3 cup sugar, salt, and Mai Tai mix. Cook in double-boiler, stirring constantly till sugar is dissolved and mixture thickens. Remove from heat; add gelatin and stir till dissolved. Mix in lemon rind and light and dark rums. Chill until mixture is slightly thickened (about 20 minutes).

Beat egg whites till stiff; continue beating as you gradually stir in remaining 1/3 cup sugar. Fold chilled gelatin mixture into egg whites. Spoon into baked pie shell. Chill till firm.

Spread Beachbum's Rum Whipped Cream (recipe on page 19) across pie. Serves 8.

We re-tooled this 1972 recipe from the C&H Sugar Company so that it actually does taste like a Mai Tai, complete with a rum-cream "float."

PAPAYA DAIQUIRI ICE

3 ripe papayas
1/2 cup sugar
3 tablespoons fresh lime juice
3 tablespoons water
3 ounces white rum

Halve papayas lengthwise, remove and discard seeds, then scoop out fruit. Chop fruit into small pieces and put in a blender with all other ingredients. Puree at high speed until smooth, about 60 seconds. Pour into saucer champagne glasses or other dessert glasses and freeze (6 hours minimum). Serves 6 to 8.

Our original creation.

PINEAPPLE WITH RUM MINT SAUCE

2 cups sugar
1 cup water
1/2 cup fresh mint leaves, tightly packed
1 teaspoon grated lemon rind
    1/2 cup white rum (West Indies or Puerto Rican)
    1/4 cup lemon juice
    One large fresh pineapple (or more for big parties*), well chilled

Combine sugar, water, mint, and lemon rind; bring the sauce to a boil, then simmer for 3 minutes. Strain the sauce; add rum and lemon juice; chill.

Cut pineapple into chunks (discarding the hard core) and drizzle sauce over it. (*You'll have enough sauce for 4 pine-apples. Store extra sauce in fridge; it'll keep a few days.)

Circa late 1950s.

Drinks

Illustration by Kevin Kidney

DAMON'S MAI TAI

2 ounces light rum
2 ounces dark rum
2 ounces unsweetened pineapple juice
2 ounces orange juice
1 ounce fresh lime juice
1 ounce orgeat syrup
1/4 ounce orange curacao

Shake in cocktail shaker full of crushed ice. Pour into two double old-fashioned glasses. Garnish each glass with lime wedge

317 No. Brand Blvd., Glendale, Calif.

and pineapple chunk speared to cocktail cherry. Serves two.

From Damon's restaurant, Glendale, California, circa 1969. You can still order this drink at Damon's, a south seas-themed steakhouse which has been in business since 1937 (when a complete steak dinner cost 60 cents). In 1918, Loyal A. Damon saw action in France as a member of the 144th Field Artillery, better known as the California Grizzlies. Upon his return he started a chain of Los Angeles candy stores, which he sold to finance the opening of Damon's.

HAVANA BANANA

3/4 ounce light rum

3/4 ounce creme de banana

4 ounces bottled pineapple-coconut juice (any brand)

Shake well with ice cubes and pour into tall glass. Garnish with cocktail cherry speared to orange slice.

MARINA DEL REY

CATERERS TO THE FAMOUS
AND THE FAMISHED

From the Warehouse restaurant, Marina Del Rey, California, circa 1970. Thirty years ago Marina Del Rey's yacht harbor boasted three waterfront Polynesian restaurants: Pieces Of Eight (see page 23), a Don The Beachcomber's, and The Warehouse -- the only one still standing. Opened by Burt Hixson (pictured), who at the age of 30 gave up a successful career as a cameraman and entered the restaurant business on the advice of John Wayne. Hixson decorated the Warehouse with travel memorabilia from the 28,000 miles he logged as a cinematographer; unfortunately, the intimate "crate booths" he designed no longer have their own dimmer controls.

HONOLULU COOLER

STERLING MOSSMAN

presents

HIS HAWAIIAN SPECTACULAR

HAWAII PAVILION, NEW YORK WORLD'S FAIR

3 ounces unsweetened pineapple juice
3/4 ounce fresh lime juice
1 1/2 ounces Southern Comfort

Pack a tall glass with crushed ice. Add ingredients and swizzle. Add more ice to fill.

From the Restaurant Of The Five Volcanos, in the 1964 New York World's Fair's Hawaii Pavilion, where diners watched "lovely girls diving into a lagoon for oysters - each guaranteed to produce a pearl." The Pavilion also housed the Lava Pit bar, the Sandwich Isle snack bar, industrial exhibits, retail shops, and Sterling Mossman's *Barefoot In Paradise*, "a sweeping spectacle of Pacific Island Peoples in a great new musical extravaganza." The entire 120,000 square-foot complex was demolished when the fair ended in 1965.

MAI-KAI BARREL O' RUM

2 ounces white Puerto Rican rum*
2 ounces dark Jamaican rum*
2 ounces fresh lime juice
2 ounces orange juice
2 ounces grapefruit juice
2 ounces Trader

Vic passion fruit syrup
  Teaspoon honey
  Splash soda
  6 dashes Angostura bitters

Heat honey until liquid, then combine with all other ingredients in cocktail shaker. Shake with plenty of ice cubes and pour into ceramic rum barrel or large snifter.

ABSOLUT OR GRANDFATHER BARREL

(*Upon request, the Mai Kai substitutes 4 ounces Absolut vodka or Old Granddad bourbon for the rum.)

By head bartender Mariano Licudine of the Mai-Kai restaurant, Fort Lauderdale, Florida, 1959. One of the select group of Polynesian palaces whose food and drink actually lived up to the level of its decor. Not only that, it's still open (see *Grog Log*, page 32).

MOLOKAI MULE

12 ounces orange juice
6 ounces fresh lime juice
6 ounces orgeat syrup
6 ounces brandy
6 ounces light rum
6 ounces Lemon Hart Demerara
rum
1/2 teaspoon
Angostura bitters

Mix well in a pitcher
full of ice cubes. Pour
into double old-fash-
ioned glasses, each gar-
nished with a pineapple
stick, mint sprig and or-
chid. Serves 6.

From the Kon Tiki res-
taurant in the Waikiki
Sheraton Hotel, Hawaii,
circa 1970s (see *Intoxica*,
page 81). The Kon Tiki
served this drink in a
souvenir Molokai Mule
mug, which you can still
find in thrift stores
throughout the main-
land.

POLYNESIAN PUNCH BOWL

1 fifth white Puerto Rican rum
5 cups unsweetened pineapple juice
3 cups fresh orange juice
1 cup fresh lemon juice
1 cup sloe gin
6 ounces Lopez canned coconut cream
5 ounces white creme de menthe
1 pint club soda
12 thin fresh pineapple slices
12 thin fresh orange slices

Mix all ingredients -- *except* club soda -- in punch bowl until everything, particularly coconut cream, is well-blended. Add a large block of ice, pineapple and orange slices, then place in fridge for about an hour for flavors to ripen. Just before serving, add soda and stir. Serves 24.

By Thomas Mario, food and drink editor of *Playboy* magazine, 1970.

QUIZAS

1/2 of a fresh ripe white peach (a regular peach will do in a pinch)

1 1/4 ounces Bacardi Gold rum

3/4 ounce grapefruit juice

1/3 ounce Trader Vic's rock candy syrup

Peel and puree peach half. Place in blender with all other ingredients and 4 ounces crushed ice. Blend at high speed for 30 seconds. Strain into cocktail glass.

A contemporary recipe by Gregor Scholl, proprietor of the Rum Trader, Berlin, Germany. A former bartender at the London Trader Vic's opened The Rum Trader in the mid-1970s; Scholl was such a devoted customer that he eventually bought the place from him. "Quizas" is Spanish for "maybe."

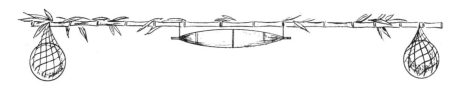

RANGOON GIMLET

1 ounce fresh lime juice
2 ounces rock candy syrup
3 ounces vodka
2 dashes Angostura bitters

Blend with 2 cups crushed ice on high speed for at least 20 seconds. Pour into cocktail glasses. Garnish each glass with lime slice and green cocktail cherry. Serves four.

From the China Trader restaurant, Burbank, California, 1963 (see *Intoxical*, page 39). Bartender Tony Ramos remembers this as TV actor Robert Conrad's favorite drink.

SATURN

1/2 ounce fresh lemon juice

1/2 ounce Trader Vic passion
fruit syrup

1/4 ounce Falernum (see page 96)

1/4 ounce orgeat syrup

1 1/4 ounces gin

Blend with 6 to 8 ounces crushed
ice until smooth. Pour into
Pilsener glass.

By J. "Popo" Galsini, 1967. Popo tended bar
at many Los Angeles Polynesian restau-
rants, predominately the Outrigger (see
Intoxica!, page 66). The Saturn won the 1967
IBA World Championship for Popo and the
California Bartenders' Guild.

Polynesian Cuisine

BILLINGSLEY'S

Outrigger

AT THE SURF AND SAND

SNEAKY TIKI

Trader Dick's
SOUTH SEA ISLAND
RESTAURANT
SPARKS, NEVADA

1 ounce fresh lemon juice

1 1/2 ounces unsweetened pineapple juice

1/3 ounce orange curacao

1/4 ounce grenadine
1 ounce light Puerto Rican rum
1 ounce dark Jamaican rum

Blend with 8 ounces crushed ice. Serve in Sneaky Tiki mug (see below) or chimney glass.

The house drink at Harvey's Top Of The Wheel, a tiki bar in Harvey's Casino Resort, Lake Tahoe, Nevada, circa 1960. "Beware of the Sneaky Tiki," warned Harvey's menu: "light enough to make you careless -- strong enough to add zest to the conversation. 'Take me home' says the mug. 'I am yours.'" Literally thousands of these tall black vessels with purple script were given away before The Top Of The Wheel closed over 30 years ago. But the Sneaky Tiki survived thanks to sneaky Dick Graves, late of Trader Dick's restaurant in Reno's Nugget casino. Graves proudly admitted stealing the recipe from Harvey's; he also copped to ripping off his dinner menu from Trader Vic, who hated Graves with a passion he normally reserved for communists and check-dodgers.

TAHITIAN LANAI RUM PUNCH

1 cup amber Virgin Islands rum (preferably Cruzan)
1/2 cup fresh pineapple, chopped fine
1/2 cup fresh banana, chopped fine
1/2 cup fresh lime juice
1 cup unsweetened pineapple juice
2 ounces fresh lemon juice
1 ounce (2 tablespoons) brown sugar

Dissolve sugar in lime juice, then put everything in blender with 5 cup capacity. Blend without ice at high speed until thoroughly mixed (around 1 minute). Empty blender into pitcher, fill pitcher to top with crushed ice, and stir until punch is well chilled. Pour into Pilsener glasses, each garnished with a Tiare (Tahiti's official flower). Serves 6.

From the Papeete Bar of the Tahitian Lanai restaurant, in the Waikikian Hotel, Hawaii, 1958 (see *Intoxica*, page 49). James Michener wrote his novel *Hawaii* in a room at the Waikikian, his favorite hotel in Oahu.

TONGA PUNCH

2 fifths light rum
1 quart fresh lemon juice (app. 20 lemons)
24 ounces (3 cups) orange juice
12 ounces brandy
12 ounces orange curacao
12 ounces Trader Vic passion fruit syrup
6 ounces grenadine

Mix well in punch bowl filled with ice. Serves 25.

Quoth Trader Vic: "This mixture is for an informal, fun-loving group of people, no holds barred." Vic changed his recipe several times over the years; this one dates from 1946.

TRADER VIC DAIQUIRI

3 ounces fresh lime juice

2 1/4 ounces grapefruit juice

3 teaspoons rock candy syrup

1 1/2 ounces maraschino liqueur

6 ounces white Puerto Rican rum

Pour all ingredients into blender (5 cup capacity). Fill blender to top with ice cubes. Blend until frappéd. Pour into cocktail glasses or saucer champagne glasses. Serves 6 to 8.

By Trader Vic, circa 1960.

TRADEWINDS

4 ounces fresh lemon juice

3 ounces Lopez canned coconut cream

3 ounces apricot brandy

3 ounces white Puerto Rican rum

3 ounces dark Jamaican rum

Pour all ingredients into blender (5 cup capacity). Fill blender to top with ice cubes. Blend until smooth. Serves 4 to 6.

A Caribbean recipe, circa 1970s.

Recipe Index

Resource Guide

HARD-TO-FIND INGREDIENTS (FOR FOOD): Dynasty brand HOISIN SAUCE, PLUM SAUCE and HOT MUSTARD are available in supermarkets, where you'll also find Geisha brand WATER CHESTNUTS and La Choy BAMBOO SHOOTS. The best CHINESE OYSTER SAUCE is marketed by Lee Kum Kee, the company that actually invented the stuff in the 19th century (log on to home.LKK.com); they also make CHAR SUI BARBECUE SAUCE. You can order WATER CHESTNUT FLOUR from www.specialfoods.com. Oetker Ltd. exports VANILLA SUGAR from Canada (www.oetker.ca/).

HARD-TO-FIND INGREDIENTS (FOR DRINKS): Trader Vic's Food Products markets ORGEAT SYRUP, PASSION FRUIT SYRUP, and ROCK CANDY SYRUP, which you can order on-line at www.tradervics.com. (You can also make your own rock candy syrup; see *Intoxica!*, page 10.) After a long absence, several brands of FALERNUM are now available - - but the only one we like is Fee Brothers (call 1-800-961-FEES for ordering info). LOPEZ COCONUT CREAM can be had at most liquor stores and supermarkets.

FURTHER READING: Oddly enough, we recommend *BEACHBUM BERRY'S GROG LOG* and *BEACHBUM BERRY'S INTOXICA!*, available through ClubTiki.com, Amazon.com, or by phone at 1-800-866-8929. See also Sven Kirsten's *THE BOOK OF TIKI* (Taschen Publishing) and Otto Von Stroheim's *TIKI NEWS* (www.tikinews.com).

FOR THE BEACHBUM LIFESTYLE: TIKI OBJECTS BY BOSKO sells tikis, tiki bars, decor, mugs, luau kits, gift sets, and more. Log on to www.tikibosko.com, or send for a mail-order catalogue by posting one dollar to PO Box 300024, Escondido, California, 92030.

CPSIA information can be obtained
at www.ICGtesting.com
Printed in the USA
BVHW041434120321
602296BV00008B/889